Yellow Journalism

by Jason Skog

Content Adviser: Donald Stewart, M.A.,
Chair, Department of Mass Communication,
Francis Marion University

Reading Adviser: Alexa L. Sandmann, Ph.D.,
Associate Professor of Literacy,
Kent State University

Compass Point Books ◆ Minneapolis, Minnesota

Compass Point Books
3109 West 50th Street, #115
Minneapolis, MN 55410

Visit Compass Point Books on the Internet at *www.compasspointbooks.com*
or e-mail your request to *custserv@compasspointbooks.com*

On the cover: An 1898 cartoon by Leon Barritt depicting the struggle between newspaper
publishers Joseph Pulitzer and William Randolph Hearst, who are dressed as the Yellow Kid

Photographs ©: Library of Congress, cover, back cover, 10, 21, 29; Prints Old & Rare, back
cover (far left); The Granger Collection, New York, 4, 7, 9, 11, 13, 16, 17, 32, 33, 39; North Wind
Picture Archives, 6, 8, 14, 26, 35; Bettmann/Corbis, 12, 23, 28, 36; Hulton Archive/Getty Images,
19; Frederic Lewis/Getty Images, 20; Courtesy of The Bancroft Library, University of California,
Berkeley, 22; Pach Brothers/Corbis, 30; Corbis, 34; James Leynse/Corbis, 40.

Managing Editor: Catherine Neitge
Page Production: Lori Bye
Photo Researcher: Svetlana Zhurkin
Cartographer: XNR Productions, Inc.
Library Consultant: Kathleen Baxter

Creative Director: Keith Griffin
Editorial Director: Carol Jones

Library of Congress Cataloging-in-Publication Data
Skog, Jason.
  Yellow journalism / by Jason Skog.
     p. cm. — (We the people)
  Includes bibliographical references and index.
  ISBN-13: 978-0-7565-2456-2 (library binding)
  ISBN-10: 0-7565-2456-3 (library binding)
  ISBN-13: 978-0-7565-3225-3 (paperback)
  ISBN-10: 0-7565-3225-6 (paperback)
1. Journalists—United States—Biography—Juvenile literature. 2. Sensationalism in journalism
—United States—History—19th century—Juvenile literature. I. Title. II. Series.
  PN4871.S57 2006
  071'.309034—dc22   2006027096

TABLE OF CONTENTS

REMEMBER THE MAINE!

In the mid-1890s, William Randolph Hearst was the rich, young publisher of the *New York Journal*. Hearst was in a fierce battle to win newspaper readers, and his chief rival was Joseph Pulitzer, publisher of the *New York World*.

Both newspapers were closely watching the island of Cuba, just 90 miles (144 kilometers) off the coast of Florida.

Publisher William Randolph Hearst and his rival went head-to-head in New York City.

Fights were raging there between the Spanish government, which controlled the island, and the Cubans, who wanted their freedom. The *New York Journal* and the *New York World* reported on the conflict—sometimes truthfully and sometimes not. They told their readers that the Spanish army had killed thousands of Cubans and that many more were dying from starvation and disease. The stories led many to wonder whether it was time for the United States to get involved.

Hearst sent reporter Richard Harding Davis and illustrator Frederic Remington to Cuba to cover the fight. When they arrived there in January 1897, however, there was not much to report. Most of the Spanish forces had been defeated. Remington sent a telegram to Hearst: "Everything is quiet. There is no trouble here. There will be no war. I wish to return."

It has been widely reported that Hearst replied: "Please remain. You furnish the pictures, and I'll furnish the war." Although it makes a great story, it is doubtful he

Frederic Remington (standing left) and Richard Harding Davis (standing top right) in 1898

really said it, and in fact, he later denied it.

A year later, on February 15, 1898, a huge explosion sank the USS *Maine*, killing 266 men. The American battleship was in the harbor at Havana, Cuba. The cause could have been an accident or it could have been a Cuban or Spanish mine. But the public —including Hearst's and Pulitzer's newspapers—quickly blamed Spanish forces. "Remember the *Maine!*" became the rallying cry of the newspapers and the public. Soon after, the United States declared war on Spain. As the war raged, Hearst bragged to readers, "How do you like the *Journal's* war?"

The message was becoming clear from reading his newspapers. Hearst wanted to see the United States come to Cuba's aid. Pulitzer's paper also made the Cuban conflict seem more exciting and dangerous than it really was.

The result was that each newspaper was selling more than 750,000 copies each day and more than a million copies on Sundays. Publishers Hearst and Pulitzer were getting richer by the minute.

The era of yellow journalism was at its peak. Truth was often stretched, and stories of crime, corruption, and scandal were used to sell newspapers.

Front page of Hearst's Journal, *February 17, 1898, two days after the USS* Maine *exploded*

7

A political cartoon depicts Joseph Pulitzer holding a press printing his New York World.

Today yellow journalism serves as a reminder to journalists and readers of the value of accurate and honest reporting and writing.

THE YELLOW KID

The main period of yellow journalism was from 1895 to 1898. The two papers that started the trend were the New York newspapers of Hearst and Pulitzer: the *Journal* and the *World*.

The term *yellow journalism* comes from a cartoon character in Pulitzer's newspaper. "Hogan's Alley" was New York's most popular comic strip. One of its main characters was Mickey Dugan, a young boy in yellow pajamas. Better known as the

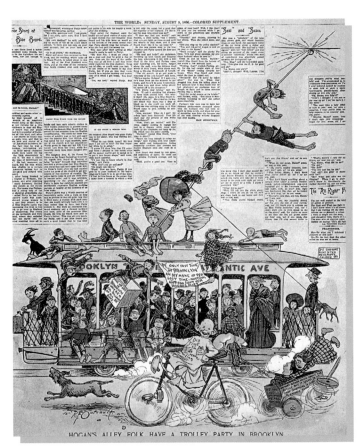

The Yellow Kid (in front) played an important role in the popular comic strip "Hogan's Alley."

Richard Outcault

Yellow Kid, he appeared in the only comic strip to run in color. He stood out in the otherwise black-and-white newspaper.

The comic was set in some of New York's poorest neighborhoods, and it often showed the Yellow Kid making fun of rich people and their hobbies. Richard Outcault, an illustrator at Pulitzer's newspaper, created "Hogan's Alley." It quickly caught Hearst's attention, and he hired Outcault away from his main competitor. Pulitzer offered Outcault more money, but Hearst won the bidding war. Eventually, Pulitzer hired a new artist who drew a comic that included a character similar to the Yellow Kid. When both papers featured two popular yellow characters, the newspapers became known as the yellow papers. And when the papers began to overstate their news reports—or make them seem more interesting or exciting than they were—the practice became known as yellow journalism.

Even before Hearst's *Journal* was blamed for pushing the

The Yellow Kid helped recruit newsboys for the New York Journal.

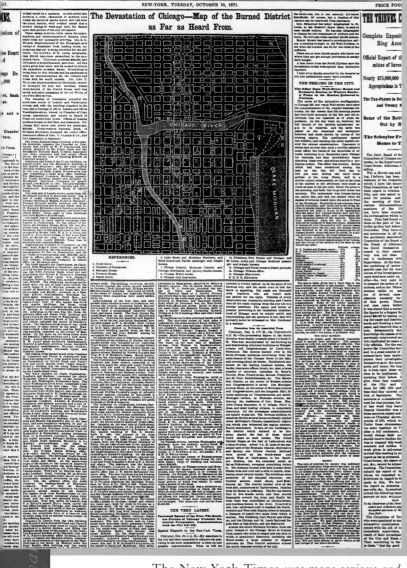

The New York Times *was more serious and restrained in its coverage of the news.*

United States into war, both of the yellow papers had disreputable reputations. The term that perhaps best describes their approach to journalism is *sensationalism*, but not in a good way. Sensational stories in newspapers were designed to produce a strong reaction from readers. They were intended to shock, excite, and entertain. This was a huge change from the more serious papers like *The New York Times* that aimed to inform and educate readers on important issues.

The yellow papers used giant headlines over stories

Huge headlines screamed the news in Hearst's New York Journal.

Reporters and illustrators converged on crime scenes to report the latest news.

involving scandal, crime, and corruption. Violence, tragedy, and gossip were also favorite topics. The writing style was aimed at working-class readers who had less education and

14

earned less money than the more typical newspaper reader.

Human-interest stories—articles with strong emotional content—also were common at the peak of yellow journalism. There were stories of mothers who died trying to rescue their children, of firefighters snatching babies from burning buildings, of seriously ill young boys selling newspapers just to survive, and of sled dogs carrying medicine to remote villages battling disease.

The *Journal* and the *World* even battled to solve mysterious murders. In one case, a body washed ashore in New York's East River. The *Journal* offered a $1,000 reward for clues to the man's identity and cause of death. Weeks later, an arrest was made and the *Journal* headline shouted: "MURDER MYSTERY SOLVED BY THE JOURNAL."

JOURNALISM GIANTS

Of the two yellow journalism giants, Joseph Pulitzer was first on the scene. He is best known as the namesake of the Pulitzer Prizes, which recognize the best in American journalism each year. Ironically, Pulitzer wasn't always known for printing the greatest journalism himself.

In fact, Pulitzer had been practicing sensational journal-

An 1896 political cartoon depicts "Atlas Joe" Pulitzer trying to influence world events with his newspaper.

ism—with reporting and writing designed more to entertain than inform—a decade before Hearst arrived in New York.

Born April 10, 1847, in Makó, Hungary, Joseph Pulitzer left home at age 17 to join the military. However, he was rejected for service by several European armies

Joseph Pulitzer

because of his poor eyesight and slight build. A U.S. Army recruiter in Hamburg, Germany, signed Pulitzer up for service, and he came to the United States to fight on the Union side in the Civil War.

At the end of the war, Pulitzer moved to St. Louis, Missouri, where there was a large German-speaking community. He studied English and became a citizen in 1867. Pulitzer wanted to be a lawyer and was admitted to the bar in 1868. That same year, he took a job on a German-language newspaper in St. Louis, the *Westliche Post*.

The next year, Pulitzer was elected a Missouri state representative. By 1872, he had made enough money to buy a part interest in the *Westliche Post*. Six years later, he bought the *St. Louis Dispatch,* the city's failing newspaper. He immediately merged it with another paper, the *Evening Post,* to create the *St. Louis Post-Dispatch*. At 31 years old, he became publisher of what remains to this day as St. Louis' major newspaper.

However, Pulitzer soon outgrew St. Louis. In 1883, he moved to New York, the center of the publishing world, and quickly bought a small and stumbling newspaper, the *New York World*. Within four years, the paper's circulation rose from 15,000 readers to more than 250,000. It

Pulitzer was depicted as the leader of liberal Republicanism in a St. Louis cartoon.

The New York World Building was once the tallest in the world. It was demolished in 1955.

wasn't long before Pulitzer was locked in a vicious battle for readers with Hearst's *Journal.*

William Randolph Hearst was born April 29, 1863, in San Francisco, California. He was the only child of a wealthy silver and copper miner. Hearst collected stamps, coins, and porcelain, and he loved visiting European art galleries. He was spoiled as a boy, and later, as a student, he was a prankster who was kicked out of Harvard University for one of his stunts.

He got his start in newspapers in San Francisco.

His father, George Hearst, owned the *San Francisco Examiner*, and William took over as its publisher in 1887, when he was just 23 years old.

At the time, the paper wasn't earning much money or attracting many readers, but Hearst was determined to make it a success. He greatly admired Joseph Pulitzer and began imitating Pulitzer's *New York World*, which was attracting attention with huge headlines and exciting—if not always entirely true—stories.

In a note to his father, Hearst promised to start "a revolution in the

William Randolph Hearst

21

George Hearst

sleepy journalism" of California. Soon Hearst was spending his father's money to increase the number of pages and expand the newspaper's staff.

He once said, "If news is wanted it often has to be sent for." In that spirit, Hearst sent reporters to jump off ferryboats to test the rescue skills of the crew, or to save fishermen who were stuck on the rocks. Hearst also hired women writers who acted as "sob sisters," writing human-interest articles and advice columns. The readership of the *Examiner* grew tremendously, but the paper lost money because of Hearst's wild spending. When George Hearst died in 1891, William did not get any of his money because his father had worried that he could not manage it.

An 1895 cartoon depicts President William McKinley trying to stop yellow journalism.

Then in 1895, Hearst's mother sold $7.5 million worth of stock in the Anaconda copper mines and gave the money to William. He could finally pursue his dream of entering the New York newspaper world. In September 1895, he bought the *New York Journal* and began competing head-to-head with Pulitzer's *World*.

YELLOW PAPER REPORTERS

Before the era of yellow journalism, being a reporter was often considered a dead-end job. The pay was low, the hours were long, and there was little glory. Reporters rarely got to put their names on their stories. Editors and publishers were the famous faces of newspapers. Pulitzer and Hearst were among the biggest stars of the newspaper world.

That began to change at the yellow papers, where writers were encouraged to tell the best stories possible, occasionally stretch the truth, and, it was hoped, sell more newspapers.

Yellow paper reporters typically came from poor, religious families, though they weren't likely to be religious themselves. Instead, they had faith in science, social progress, and American inventiveness. They were not happy just writing about the news. They would rather solve crimes or join the rush to Alaska in search of gold.

Reporters wanted to affect government policy or

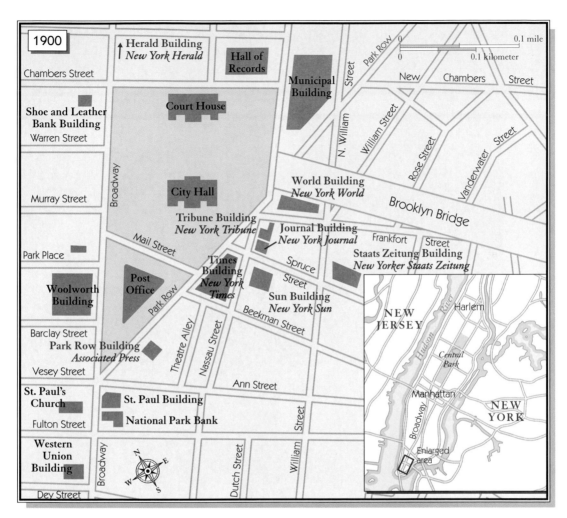

New York City's newspaper buildings were grouped together near Park Row.

prompt social change, and they had tremendous energy. One reporter sent on a six-week assignment in Alaska returned with more than 30,000 words and 3,000 photographs. That's enough words to fill 10 books like this one.

25

Reporters started gaining prominence in the late 1880s.

Two of the best reporters became superstars: Nellie Bly and Richard Harding Davis.

Nellie Bly was America's most famous female journalist in the decade leading up to the main yellow journalism years. Elizabeth Cochrane, who used the pen name Nellie Bly, worked for the *New York World*. On her first assignment, in September 1887, Bly acted mentally disturbed so she would be admitted to an insane asylum. "INSIDE THE MAD HOUSE" was the resulting article's headline. The article led to a formal investigation of the asylum's terrible conditions, and she later published a book on the subject.

Another time, Bly pretended to be a recent immigrant looking for work, taking jobs in factories to expose the terrible working conditions. She was so successful, and her stories had such impact, that women wrote, "For God's sake, send Nellie Bly. She can do anything."

It was Pulitzer's decision to send Bly on a trip that won her international fame. The goal was to beat the time it took Phileas Fogg—a fictitious character from a Jules Verne novel called *Around the World in 80 Days*—to travel around the globe. When Nellie Bly crossed the finish line, it had taken her a record-setting 72 days, 6 hours, and 11 minutes.

The *World* published stories from her stops along the way, and the trip was turned into a board game. There were

Nellie Bly's around-the-world trip was front-page news in the World.

songs about the famous voyage. Bly was bigger than life.

She went on to write many stories, especially about women's rights and social reforms. She was working for Hearst's *Journal* when she died of pneumonia in 1922 at age 57. Her last editor, Arthur Brisbane, said that in her prime, Bly was "the best reporter in America, and that is saying a good deal."

Elizabeth Cochrane was better known as Nellie Bly.

Perhaps the only other newspaper reporter of the time who could compare to Nellie Bly in popularity and ability was Richard Harding Davis.

Richard Harding Davis wrote exciting and colorful news stories from around the world.

Davis got his start at two Philadelphia papers, and his writing style helped him get a job as a reporter for the *New York Sun*. As his popularity grew and his writing style blossomed, Davis attracted the attention of Hearst, who hired him for $500 to cover a single college football game. It was an incredible amount of money at the time, but Hearst was battling Pulitzer for readers, and Davis already had a following.

At a time when most reporters were hard-drinking, foul-mouthed, and spirited, Davis was sober, nicely dressed, and ambitious. He covered college sports and crime and wrote short stories, travel pieces, novels, and plays.

It was his war reporting at the turn of the century, though, that made him famous. There was rarely a conflict, war, or battle around the globe that he didn't visit and write about. He represented the romance and excitement that came with the job.

When Hearst sent him to cover the Cuban crisis, Davis felt the United States should come to the aid of the Cuban rebels. His stories helped nudge the American public

Davis (right) interviewed war hero and future president Teddy Roosevelt in Cuba in 1898.

to his view, and soon the country was at war with Spain.

Davis died of heart disease in 1916, a week shy of his 52nd birthday. H.L. Mencken of the *Baltimore Sun* called Davis "the hero of our dreams."

THE BRIGHT SIDE

Beyond the scary headlines and gory illustrations of the yellow papers, there was also some solid journalism being done by talented writers and thoughtful editors. Hearst

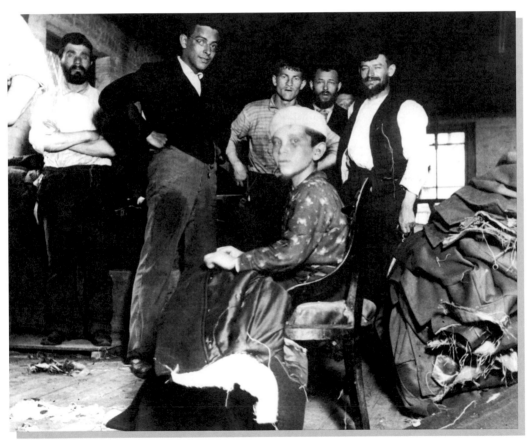

Newspapers helped expose the horrible working conditions of child laborers in the 1800s.

himself referred to yellow journalism as "journalism that acts," particularly when it involved investigative stories that exposed corruption. While both the *Journal* and the *World* were known for rooting out wrongdoing, Pulitzer's paper was the first to do it so well and so often.

Besides revealing the poor treatment of patients at a

Investigative stories brought to light the brutal living conditions of the poor.

mental hospital, the *World* ran a series of stories on insurance companies that led to an investigation by the government. It exposed poor working conditions in the clothing and cigarette industries, shady campaign contributions, and bribery and corruption in all levels of government.

Pulitzer's legacy lives on today in the annual Pulitzer Prizes, the highest honor American journalists can receive.

On the day Hearst's *Journal* wrote about the capture of the chief suspect in the murder of the

Readers eagerly bought newspapers as soon as they were printed and delivered.

35

man who had washed ashore, guards were hired to protect the newspaper delivery wagons. Eager readers swarmed the delivery crews, desperate to read the conclusion of the story.

People couldn't get enough of this style of journalism. As the circulation of the yellow papers swelled, newspapers

A crowd watched for news announcements at the New York Tribune *building in 1898.*

36

throughout the country copied the formats. In every large city, the "yellowest" paper almost always had the largest circulation. More traditional papers scoffed at the sensational approach. Hearst and Pulitzer claimed they were just giving the public what it wanted. However, as more and more papers adopted startling headlines and sensational news, the *World* and the *Journal* had a harder time standing out.

Eventually, Hearst and Pulitzer toned down their papers. Pulitzer even declared that the *World* would no longer stretch the truth, and Hearst's *Journal* started to act more professionally. By the turn of the century, it seemed the era of yellow journalism was ending.

LESSONS LEARNED

While some still debate the value of the yellow papers, their presence forced other newspapers to look at the work they were doing and determine how they could attract and hold readers—responsibly.

The term yellow journalism reflects an era and is rarely used to describe modern news media. Today's industry is far too big and complex for such an old term. Now critics have new phrases to describe journalism that is sensational, inflammatory, slanted, unfair, or inaccurate.

They include:

- Tabloid journalism, with its massive headlines on shocking stories, often about celebrities;

- Corporate journalism, in which large companies are suspected of running stories that will help profits, but not those that might harm profits; and

- Media bias, in which articles aim to persuade readers on an issue.

50 Cents

THE YELLOW KID

IN

McFADDEN'S FLATS

BY

E.W. TOWNSEND
AUTHOR OF
"CHIMMIE FADDEN"

AND

R.F. OUTCAULT
CREATOR OF THE
"YELLOW KID"

G·W·DILLINGHAM·Co.
PUBLISHERS
·NEW·YORK·

DIS
BOOK iS
DE STORY
OF ME
SWEET
YOVNG
LIFE

The Yellow Kid represented a key chapter in journalism history.

Journalism school graduates represent a new generation of reporters and editors.

Today virtually every newspaper tries to be accurate, fair, and honest. While there will probably always be some accusations of biased reporting and unfair treatment, such disputes often arise from political disagreements. Many newspapers have strict ethics and accuracy policies that reporters and editors sign. In doing so, they pledge not to have any conflicts that could cloud their judgment and not to let their personal views color their stories.

Before his death, Pulitzer gave money to Columbia University in New York to build one of the nation's first journalism schools. When it opened in 1912, college students could take courses to prepare themselves for newspaper work. Today Columbia and dozens of other universities offer courses in newspaper, television, and radio journalism. They focus on writing, editing, design, and ethics. The programs also include journalism history, teaching students about Hearst, Pulitzer, and yellow journalism.

GLOSSARY

circulation—the average number of copies of a newspaper or magazine sold

corruption—willingness to do things that are wrong or illegal to get money, favors, or power

disreputable—having a bad reputation

immigrant—a person who moves from one country to live permanently in another

inflammatory—tending to cause anger or disorder

investigation—an official examination to find information

namesake—one who is named after another or for whom another person or thing is named

scandal—an action that offends people and causes disgrace

DID YOU KNOW?

- In 1902, William Randolph Hearst was elected to the U.S. Congress representing New York. In 1904, he lost a bid to run for president but was re-elected to Congress. In 1906, he ran for governor of New York. He lost a close race and later ran for mayor of New York, a race he also lost. In 1910, he ran for lieutenant governor of New York and lost. That was his last bid for office.

- Joseph Pulitzer served briefly in Congress in 1885 and early 1886, but realized he could have more influence as the publisher of his newspaper.

- As Pulitzer grew older, he became extremely sensitive to the quietest noise. Even the sound of crumpling newspaper caused him terrible pain. He had a soundproof chamber built in his house, and he often communicated with his newspaper office via notes and telegrams.

- At the peak of his career, Hearst owned 26 daily newspapers across the country, 11 Sunday papers, a syndication service, a Sunday supplement, six magazines, several radio stations, and a movie studio.

IMPORTANT DATES

Timeline

1883	Joseph Pulitzer purchases the *New York World* newspaper.
1889	Nellie Bly begins her journey around the world, which takes her 72 days, 6 hours, and 11 minutes.
1895	The Yellow Kid cartoon first appears in the *New York World;* William Randolph Hearst purchases the *New York Journal* newspaper, providing Pulitzer's first real challenge.
1896	Hearst hires Richard F. Outcault, the Yellow Kid cartoonist, away from Pulitzer's *World* and gives him a high-paying job at the *Journal;* cartoonist George Luks continues to draw a Yellow Kid at the *World*.
1898	An explosion kills 266 men and sinks the USS *Maine*, an American battleship in a Cuban harbor; the United States declares war on Spain.

IMPORTANT PEOPLE

WILLIAM RANDOLPH HEARST (1863–1951)

Newspaper publisher, owner of several magazines, radio stations, and a movie studio who was one of America's wealthiest men; a fictionalized version of his life was made into the movie Citizen Kane, *which many consider one of the best movies ever made*

WILLIAM MCKINLEY (1843–1901)

U.S. president who declared war on Spain shortly after the sinking of the USS Maine; *historians say he never read the* New York Journal, *which claimed it started the war*

RICHARD F. OUTCAULT (1863–1928)

Creator of the "Hogan's Alley" Yellow Kid character and pioneer of the modern comic strip; he went on to create Buster Brown, a drawing of a young boy whose image later was licensed to sell the Buster Brown brand of shoes and other consumer products

JOSEPH PULITZER (1847-1911)

Newspaper publisher and founder of the Columbia School of Journalism whose endowment established the Pulitzer Prizes; at the end of his career, he was one of the most respected journalists in the country despite his period of yellow journalism

WANT TO KNOW MORE?

At the Library

Bentley, Nancy, and Donna Guthrie. *The Young Journalist's Book: How to Write and Produce Your Own Newspaper.* Brookfield, Conn.: Millbrook Press, 1998.

Cohen, Daniel. *Yellow Journalism: Scandal, Sensationalism, and Gossip in the Media.* Brookfield, Conn.: Twenty-first Century Books, 2000.

Frazier, Nancy. *William Randolph Hearst: Modern Media Tycoon.* Woodbridge, Conn.: Blackbirch Press, 2001.

Whitelaw, Nancy. *Joseph Pulitzer and the New York World.* Greensboro, N.C.: Morgan Reynolds Publishing, 2000.

On the Web

For more information on this topic, use FactHound.

1. Go to *www.facthound.com*

2. Type in this book ID: 0756524563

3. Click on the *Fetch It* button.

FactHound will find the best Web sites for you.

On the Road

The Newseum
Corner of Pennsylvania Avenue
and Sixth Street N.W.
Washington, DC
888/639-7386
An interactive museum with exhibits
on important events and people in
journalism

Hearst Castle at San Simeon
750 Hearst Castle Road
San Simeon, CA 93452-9740
800/927-2020
William Randolph Hearst's elaborate
home, a state historical monument
that is open for tours

Look for more We the People books about this era:

The American Newsboy

Angel Island

The Great Chicago Fire

Great Women of the Suffrage
    Movement

The Harlem Renaissance

The Haymarket Square Tragedy

The Hindenburg

Industrial America

The Johnstown Flood

The Lowell Mill Girls

The Orphan Trains

Roosevelt's Rough Riders

Women of the Harlem Renaissance

A complete list of We the People titles is available on our Web site:
www.compasspointbooks.com

INDEX

About the Author

Jason Skog is a writer who lives in Brooklyn, New York, with his wife and son. He has been a newspaper writer for 12 years, covering education, the legal system, city government, technology, and youth issues. His work has appeared in magazines and newspapers, including *The New York Times,* the *Boston Globe,* and the *Baltimore Sun.* This is his fourth book for young readers.